Genre Realistic Fiction

I0800771

Essential Question
How can we take responsibility?

The Go-Kart

by Adrienne Jansen • illustrated by John Batten

Chapter 1
The Big Mess 2

Chapter 2
Time to Build 6

Chapter 3
The Drill 9

Chapter 4
The Race 13

Respond to Reading 16

PAIRED READ **Board Lesson** 17

Focus on Literary Elements 20

Chapter 1

The Big Mess

Katie and Chelsea looked at each other with puzzled expressions. There was so much noise coming from the yard that they could barely talk, so finally they went to see what was happening. Katie opened the back door and saw her brother, Kyle. He was building something complicated made out of wood, pipes, and plastic.

"What is that **contraption**?" she asked.

"I'm building a go-kart for the competition at school. Richie and I are definitely going to win."

A pipe fell off the go-kart and landed on the grass.

Katie laughed and said, "You won't even get that big mess to the race. I could make a better go-kart than that."

"I bet you can't," Kyle said.

Later that day, Katie and Chelsea were reading in Katie's bedroom. Katie couldn't stop thinking about the go-kart competition.

"Hey, Chelsea, I have an idea," she said finally. "Let's build a go-kart and enter the race."

Chelsea snorted and said, "We don't know anything about go-karts."

"Kyle doesn't know that much either, but he's building one anyway," Katie said.

Chelsea felt doubtful but she didn't say no. Katie started talking again before Chelsea could refuse. "We just need a team and a plan. We should ask Melita to be on our team."

"Melita doesn't like teams," Chelsea argued.

"That's true, but Melita is really good with computers. She could help us find an awesome go-kart plan on the Internet."

The next day after school, Katie and Chelsea talked to Melita about their idea. They asked if she would help them find a plan on the Internet.

"You're a computer whiz. Mr. Kirk asked you to come to the teachers' **lounge** when they needed help with the computer," Katie pointed out.

"We need you on our team," Chelsea added.

Melita felt unsure about joining a team, but finally she smiled and agreed.

That night Melita and her mom looked for go-kart plans on the Internet. Her mom was an engineer, so she knew how to build things.

"What kind of go-kart do you want?" Melita's mom asked. "What will make it go?"

"Someone sits in it and steers and two people push it. But it needs to look cool," Melita said. "Maybe it could have a classic design and be made out of wood. I think I'll search for 'vintage go-kart plans.' Is 'vintage' the right word?"

Her mom nodded and said, "That's a wonderful idea. I bet you'll find a plan the others will love."

Melita typed the words into the search engine, and she and her mom clicked on links until they found the perfect plan. They thought the design looked great, and the Web site listed all the tools and materials they needed.

STOP AND CHECK

Why do Katie and Chelsea ask Melita to help them?

Chapter 2
Time to Build

After school on Wednesday, the three girls met in Chelsea's yard. Katie's uncle Jeff was **renovating** his house. They were lucky that he was fixing it up because he was able to give them some lumber. Chelsea's mom had given them some wheels and axles from a stroller she was throwing out. And they had borrowed tools from Chelsea's uncle Keith, who lived next door.

"You can borrow my tools, but take good care of them," Uncle Keith had said.

The girls quickly got to work. At the end of the day, Melita said, "We have to put the tools away. Chelsea's uncle said to take care of them."

"That's your job," Chelsea said. "I'll clean up the yard."

On Thursday, Melita's mom helped them nail the boards to make the bottom and sides of the go-kart. On Friday, Katie's uncle Jeff helped them put together the wheels and axles. Suddenly, he stopped working and looked **perplexed**. The girls weren't sure why he was confused.

"You don't have the right kind of bolt for the front wheels," Uncle Jeff said. "The bolts need to be in **proportion** to the axle. These are too small, so you'll have to go to the hardware store in the morning."

The go-kart was almost finished by the next morning. "We just need to paint it and attach the front wheels," Katie said.

"Let's paint it now so it'll be dry when we get back from the hardware store," Melita said.

The girls painted the outside of the go-kart bright blue and the inside bright yellow. Then they stood back to admire their creation. It looked like a winner!

Now all they had to do was buy the bolts for the front wheels. They asked Chelsea's dad to drive them to the hardware store.

Chelsea knew how important the tools were to Uncle Keith, so she suggested putting them away.

"We don't have time," Katie said impatiently. "We'll put the tools away when we get back."

STOP AND CHECK

Why don't the girls put the tools away before they go to the store?

Chapter 3
The Drill

When they returned from the store, Chelsea's dad said, "We need to drill a hole to attach these bolts. Chelsea, please hand me the drill."

Chelsea looked around the yard, but the tools were gone! "Do you think someone stole them?" she asked. She began to feel frightened.

Then she turned to Katie and said, "You said not to put the tools away, so it's your fault they were stolen."

Katie did not think that was fair. "We didn't have time," she responded. "You borrowed them, so they are your responsibility."

Chelsea decided to blame Melita. "It's not my fault. It's Melita's job to put the tools away."

Melita got angry. "It's not my fault, either!"

Chelsea's dad frowned and said, "Stop arguing. You have to tell Uncle Keith that you lost his tools."

Chelsea's dad went back into the house. The girls glared at each other. They couldn't finish the go-kart without a drill, but no one wanted to accept blame for the missing tools.

Katie knew they wouldn't get to race, and she was disappointed. "It's your fault that we won't be champions," she said to Chelsea.

Chelsea sat down and folded her arms. "No, it's your fault," she said angrily.

They were still **grousing** at each other when Uncle Keith's daughter, Jessica, walked up.

"Hey, what are you arguing about?" Jessica asked.

All three girls started talking at once, each of them blaming someone else for the missing tools. Jessica asked if they were sure that the tools were stolen.

"They were here when we left, and they're gone now!" Katie said.

STOP AND CHECK

Why does Katie think it's Chelsea's fault that the tools are missing?

"I think I know what happened. I'll be right back," Jessica said, and she ran back to her house.

"This is a disaster," Melita said. She had enjoyed being on the team when the project was going well, but now that there was a problem she wished she hadn't joined the team.

Soon Jessica was back. "You guys are in big trouble," she said. "Dad saw his tools all over the yard, so he took them back. You'll have to go apologize if you want to borrow the tools again."

"You should go because he's your uncle," Katie said to Chelsea.

"No, all three of you should go," Jessica said. "You're a team, which means you're all responsible for what happened, and you're all **answerable** to my dad."

Each girl apologized to Uncle Keith. He thought for a moment, and then he thanked them for apologizing. "It was your **obligation** to take care of my tools, girls," he said, "and you promised that you would."

In a small voice, Chelsea asked if they could borrow the drill again.

Uncle Keith agreed to give them another chance, but first he warned them to be more responsible. "Bring the drill back to me right after the race," he **cautioned**.

STOP AND CHECK

How does Jessica help the girls solve their problem?

Chapter 4

The Race

As soon as they'd tightened the bolts to **secure** the front wheels, the girls began running toward the school. They pushed the go-kart **frantically** along the road. They were worried and rushing because it was nearly time for the race to start.

They got to the school just after the race began. Chelsea took her bike helmet out of her bag, quickly put it on Melita's head, and pulled the strap tight.

"Come on, team, I know we can do it!" Chelsea said.

Soon the go-kart was flying down the track. Chelsea and Katie pushed smoothly, and Melita steered around the corners easily. They had started late, but they were catching up fast. When they passed Kyle, his mouth fell open in surprise.

FINISH

There were only five go-karts ahead of them when the crowd suddenly cheered. The first go-kart had crossed the finish line. The girls finished the race and fell onto the grass, exhausted.

Then the principal gave out the prizes. "The prize for the best-built go-kart goes to Katie, Chelsea, and Melita!" the principal announced.

The three friends jumped up and hugged each other, and then they ran to claim their prize.

Half an hour later, Chelsea set the drill down on Uncle Keith's kitchen counter. Katie gave him the box of chocolates they'd won.

"These are for you, to say sorry and thanks."

"I think we should share the chocolates," Uncle Keith said. "They're a prize for a champion team who learned a big lesson."

STOP AND CHECK

What lesson does Uncle Keith suggest the girls have learned?

Respond to Reading

Summarize

Use important details from *The Go-Kart* to summarize what the girls learned. Your graphic organizer may help you.

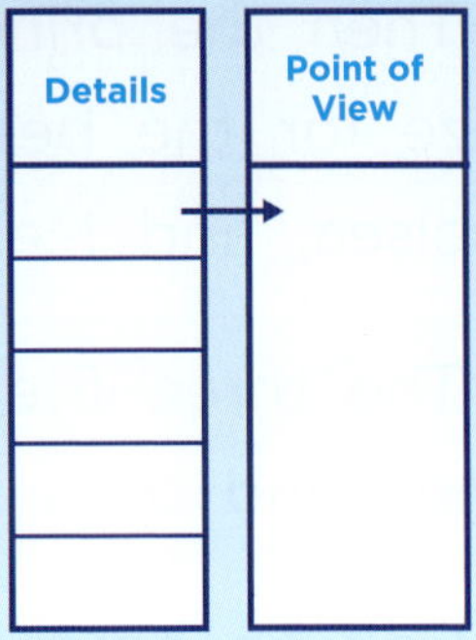

Text Evidence

1. From what point of view is this story told? Use examples from the text to help you answer. **POINT OF VIEW**

2. Find the word *refuse* on page 3. What clues help you to figure out the word's meaning? **VOCABULARY**

3. Write about the argument on pages 9 and 10. How does the point of view help you understand what happens? **WRITE ABOUT READING**

Genre Poetry

Compare Texts

Read a poem about doing the right thing.

Board Lesson

Matt wants to skate, but your board is broken.
"You can borrow my brother's," Matt says.

Matt's already flying on his board.
But this board's not yours—it feels strange.
You do a couple of gentle turns, some simple stuff.
You do a little ollie—yes! It's good.
Now you start to get a bit of speed.
You watch the gray blur racing on the ground.
You feel the wind slither across your skin.

You follow Matt up the ramp. But now you remember
this board's not yours. You're feeling nervous,
and halfway through,
you know that you won't make it.
The board goes one way.
You go the other.
Nothing hurts—you're lucky—but the board
has lost a wheel, the bolt has sheared clean through.

You'll hide the board, you'll tell him someone stole it.
You'll tell him someone else broke it.
Matt skates on over, sits beside you.
"Broke the bolt. That's bad luck, but it happens.
We'll go to the skate shop and replace it.
I've got some money—you can pay me back."

Illustration: Robin Lawrie

He's right. You know it. You could never hide it or pretend another kid should take the blame. You'd always feel guilty, and Matt's brother would know it anyway and never trust you.

With a new bolt, the skateboard's good as ever. Matt flies up over that ramp, but you don't follow. You ride the board easily around the curve, then stop.

Make Connections

What made the speaker in "Board Lesson" decide to do the right thing? **ESSENTIAL QUESTION**

Compare how the characters in *The Go-Kart* and "Board Lesson" took responsibility. **TEXT TO TEXT**

Illustration: Robin Lawrie

Focus on Literary Elements

Alliteration "Board Lesson" is a poem written in free verse. Free verse doesn't have to rhyme. However, the poet may add a rhyme from time to time. Sometimes the poet might use alliteration to help create a rhythm. Alliteration means the poet repeats the first sound in a group of words. For example, the *p* sound is repeated in "Peter Piper picked a peck of pickled peppers."

Read and Find In the poem "Board Lesson", the poet has used alliteration. For example, look at the first two lines on page 17. The *b* sound is repeated four times in "... your board is broken. 'You can borrow my brother's.'"

Your Turn

Work with a partner. Take turns reading the poem aloud and listening to each other. Listen for examples of alliteration. Each time you find one, write down the words that are close together and have the same beginning sound. What feeling does alliteration give to the words and the lines?